HOW TO PLAY THE FLUTE

A Beginner's Guide to Learning
the Flute Basics, Reading Music,
and Playing Songs

Table of Contents

Chapter 1

Introduction

Congratulations on your decision to learn to play the flute! Choosing an instrument can often be a tricky process, but you have chosen to learn one of the best. The flute is one of the most versatile instruments, appearing in bands, orchestras, and ensembles worldwide. This book will teach you everything you need to know to make your first sounds, develop a solid musical foundation, and begin playing music on your flute.

A Brief History of the Flute

The flute is one of the oldest musical instruments, with its original creation dating back to 900 B.C., and perhaps even earlier. The flute originated in many different varieties, with each culture having its own unique version. They were most commonly called transverse flutes, cross flutes, flauto traverso, or recorders. The transverse flute was first created by the Sumerians and Egyptians, who would cut a few finger holes into bamboo pipes to create their instruments. The Ancient Greeks played their flutes from the top end of the pipe, like a recorder. As time progressed the flute was considered to be an instrument of the common man, whereas the "aulos" (the descendent of the oboe) was considered to be a rich man's instrument.

The Middle Ages brought further development to the flute. For the first time, flutes were made by carving 6 finger holes into a piece of wood. Most flutes were now transverse flutes, which were held horizontally like they are today. Flute players in the Middle Ages were highly regarded, often performing in court or military ceremonies accompanied by a drum.

Ensembles began to form for the first time in the 16th century. The most common ensembles consisted of either three flutes (called a flute consort), or multiple different instruments (called broken consorts). Flutes were often the only woodwind instrument found in these consorts.

The flute rapidly gained popularity during the Baroque Period, when it became one of the main instruments heard in music. The 17th Century brought the first major change in the flute's structure: its body was divided up into three parts. The three parts of the flute consisted of a head joint, a body containing six finger holes, and a foot joint with one additional finger hole. These innovations are thought to originate from a French family, the Hotteterres. This 3-part design made its first major appearance in the performance of Jean-Baptiste Lully's opera orchestra.

The Hotteterres flute marks the beginning of the transition to the flute structure we know today. Johann J. Quantz, a Prussian Flute teacher and composer, studied the flute extensively during this time. He took note of the intonation issues that its design presented and experimented with various additions and structures for the instrument. He eventually became a flute maker himself. His improvements, along with the publication of his book containing over 400 songs for the flute, helped propel its popularity.

By the end of the 18th Century, the flute was primarily seen in classical orchestras. More keys were added to its design, and the foot joint was further developed. During the Romantic Period, Theobald Boehm redesigned the instrument, varying the sizes of key holes to match different tonalities. He arranged the holes in order to best achieve the desired acoustics, rather than ease of finger placement.

The new Boehm flute appeared at the World Exhibition in Paris in 1855, causing it to quickly gain popularity. Modern flutes today are still created using Boehm's design, with only a few modifications. The structure of the flute has come a long way since its original bamboo structure. Its presence throughout history is a testament to the flute's importance and versatility throughout all music.

Chapter 2
Flute Anatomy and Basic Care

Topics Covered

- Parts of the flute

- How to put your flute together

- How sound is produced

- Tuning your flute

- Basic care for your flute

While the flute looks fairly simple once it's all put together, opening the case for the first time can be a bit overwhelming. This chapter will teach you the basics of your flute; how to put all the parts together, how it creates sound, and what you need to know to keep it in good condition.

Parts of the Flute

Even though it is one of the smallest instruments, there are quite a few different parts that come together to make the flute work. The three main parts of the flute are fairly obvious to distinguish, and each part is made up of an intricate system of keys, pads, screws and springs.

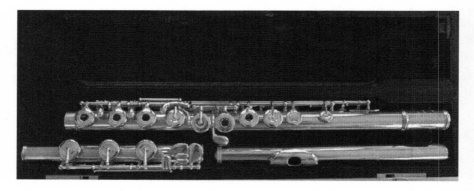

Body: The body of the flute is the longest of its three parts. It contains the majority of the keys and holes on the flute. This part of the flute is what allows the musician to produce different tones and pitches on the instrument. The keys, tone holes, pads, springs and screws intricately work together in the body of the flute. Most commonly, the body of a flute is made out of metal. Beginner level flutes are sometimes made from alloys of nickel. Advanced flutes are often plated with silver or gold, and in some cases are made entirely out of silver or gold. Less commonly, flutes can be made out of wood, which produce a very different sound. The keys on the flute are either open or closed hole. Open holed keys have a small hole in the center of the key. Most beginner level flutes are made up entirely of closed hole keys, while many intermediate and advanced level flutes contain open hole keys.

This is an open hole key.   This is a closed hole key.

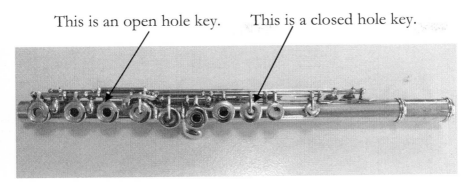

Head Joint: The head joint of the flute is the smooth part; it contains only one hole (an embouchure hole) and a circular lip plate. The head joint connects to the body of the flute and is where the sound is produced. Air is blown directly across the top of the embouchure hole into the head joint to create resonance and establish a sound from the instrument. Head joints are most often made out of metal, and advanced level head joints are sometimes made entirely of silver or gold. Occasionally, head joints are made out of wood. These wooden head joints are sometimes used with a metal body and foot joint to create an earthier sound.

Lip Plate   Embouchure Hole

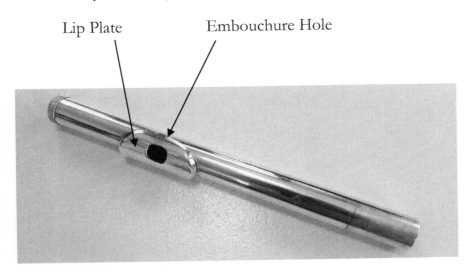

Foot Joint: The foot joint is the part of the flute that is shortest in length. It contains a few keys and holes, but not as many as the body. The foot joint connects to the bottom end of the body to complete the instrument. The keys on this part of the flute are played using the pinky finger of the musician's right hand. The foot joint contains keys, tone holes, springs, pads and screws, just like the body. It is most frequently made out of metal. There are two types of flute foot joints: a C foot and a B foot. The C foot joint is standard on beginner level flutes. It is slightly shorter, and contains only two circular keys. The C foot joint allows the musician to play down to a concert C pitch. The B foot joint is more advanced; it is slightly longer, and contains three circular keys as opposed to two. It allows the musician to play down to a concert B pitch.

Below is an example of a B foot joint – containing 3 circular keys.

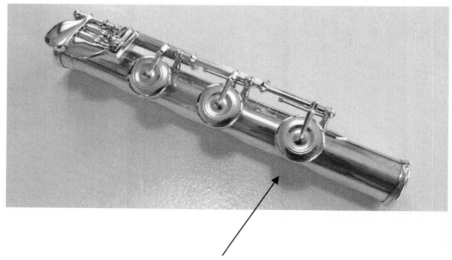

A C foot joint does not have this third key.

Keys: The keys on the flute are what allow a player to cover and open the different holes. Most keys on the flute are made out of metal, and advanced flute keys often contain silver plating. The keys come in two varieties, either open hole or closed hole. All beginner level flutes have closed holed keys. Open holed keys are commonly seen on intermediate and advanced level flutes. These keys each have a small hole in the middle of them. When a key is not depressed, the small open holes allow the flute to sound more resonate and full.

Pads: Pads are found underneath each key on the flute that covers a hole. They are usually made with either a plastic or cardboard base, and are sized to fit the key exactly. These pads are usually off-white in color, and allow for a complete covering of the hole when the key is pushed down. These pads absorb sound, efficiently blocking air from escaping if the key is depressed. Pads on the flute will need to be replaced after multiple years of use. Once they get worn down, the pads turn a dingy yellow color and appear flat and firm when pressed. When the pads are too old, they allow for extra air to escape - thus making it harder for the player to create a resonate sound.

Cork: There is not much cork visible on the flute, but it does appear in a few places. Cork can be found underneath the trill keys on the flute (the small, raised oval shaped keys on the right side of the body). The cork prevents the metal of the keys from touching the body of the flute when the trill key is used. Cork can also be found inside the top of the head joint. This cork can be adjusted slightly for tuning purposes, and serves to stop sound waves from escaping the head joint on this end.

Trill Keys (cork underneath)

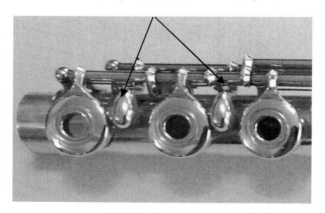

Springs: The springs on a flute are essential for it to function. Springs can be found behind every key on the flute, and they look like a skinny, straight wire. The springs are only a few centimeters in length and are held in place by a tiny metal hook on one end. If these springs ever fall out of place or are on the wrong side of the hook, the key will not spring up when they player releases pressure on it. Springs are the most common cause of flute malfunction.

Springs

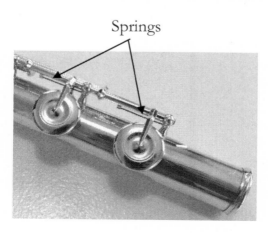

Screws: The flute contains a few screws, with the most notable found at the ends of the long rod holding the keys in place on the flute body. These screws keep the metal rod from moving, which is important since to keep the keys in their proper position.

How to Put Your Flute Together

In order to play the flute, you will need to assemble all three parts together. The body is the center of the flute. Begin by taking the body out of the case. You will need to position it with the keys facing away from you, so the L shaped key (the Ab key) is pointing away from you. The brand of flute is often engraved on the top of the body, which should be on your left side.

Brand Engraving   Ab key

Next, you will need to take out your head joint. The head joint completes the top of the flute – it fits inside the left side of the body (where the engraving appears). Carefully insert the open end of the head joint into the opening on the left side of the body. When you first put your flute together, you will want to insert the head joint all the way until it stops. Once this is done, you will need to align the embouchure hole on the head joint with the first key on the body.

The hole on the head joint should form a straight line with the first key that appears on the body.

Finally, take the foot joint out of the case. The foot joint attaches to the right side of the body, the lower end of the flute. You will need to insert the right side of the body into the side of the foot joint where the keys appear. Make sure the two are fully connected, inserting the body all the way. Then you will need to align the metal rod on the foot joint so it is in the center of the last key on the body. This will tilt the foot joint, so the keys lie at an angle.

When it's all put together, your flute will look something like this:

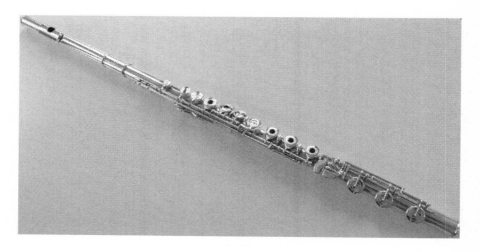

How Sound is Produced

Musical instruments require vibration to move air and create sound waves. Singers produce sound through vibrating vocal chords. Clarinets use reeds to create vibration, stringed instruments vibrate their strings, and brass instruments (like the trumpet) produce sound when the player vibrates their lips. The flute is unique from these instruments in the way it produces sound.

Sound is produced in the head joint of the flute. The player places their lower lip on the lip plate, centers it, and covers approximately one third of the hole with their lower lip. When the player blows air into the flute, the pressure in the embouchure hole sends vibrations into the body and foot joint of the flute. These vibrations reach different tone holes and send sound waves back to the head joint of the flute. The sound waves vibrate with different frequencies to create different pitches.

When more holes are covered on the flute, the air travels farther, therefore vibrating slower. These slower vibrations create lower pitches. When less holes are covered, the air travels a shorter distance and vibrates faster. This creates higher pitches.

Tuning Your Flute

Instruments that are higher in pitch are often the most important to tune, as their tone frequencies vary the most. Since the flute is the highest pitched instrument in a band and orchestra (along with the violin), they usually require the most frequent intonation adjustments.

Luckily, tuning the flute is fairly simple. To tune your flute, you will simply need to adjust your head joint by pulling it out or pushing it in. Even the slightest adjustment can cause a large difference in pitch, so make sure to only pull or push the head joint with very small movements at a time. Most flutes are not made to be in tune with the head joint pushed all the way in. Whenever you adjust your head joint, make sure that the embouchure hole is still properly aligned and centered with the first key on the flute. You may need to roll it slightly in or out in order to comfortably make a sound, but a general rule is that the embouchure hole and first key should be relatively in line with one another.

When two instruments play the same concert pitch, the note they produce may still vary slightly from one another. This is where tuning becomes important. Before you play your flute, it is important to check your intonation. You can do so with a tuner or by matching pitch with another instrument. It is recommended that you either purchase a tuner or download a tuner app on your phone (there are many free options). Tuning by ear is an advanced skill that requires a great deal of practice. The best tuning note for the flute is either A or Bb.

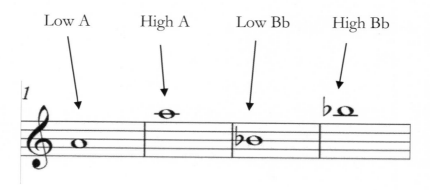

When tuning your instrument, you will need to hold your tuning note out for a few counts. This will allow your ear and/or the tuner to get an accurate reference of the sound. It is best to begin tuning with the low pitch first (either low A or low Bb). If you are using a tuner, your tuner will light up to let you know if the pitch you are playing is sharp, flat, or right on.

Listening Example #1: Tuning Notes
https://soundcloud.com/jason_randall/sets/how-to-play-the-flute

In track 1, listen to the four tuning notes on the flute: low A, high A, low Bb and high Bb. Pay special attention to the length of each note to get a feel for how long you'll want to hold each tuning note when you play for the tuner.

If your tuning note is slightly higher than it should be, the tuner will tell you that it is sharp. When your flute is sharp, you will need to pull the head joint out. Remember to do this slightly, only in small increments. Gently pull the head joint out of the body. Play your note again for the tuner and adjust further if necessary. You may need to make several small adjustments until your note is in tune.

If your flute is slightly lower than it should be, the tuner will tell you that it is flat. When your flute is flat, you will need to push the head joint in slightly. This should also be done using small, gentle adjustments. Play your tuning note again after you've made an adjustment. Once your lower notes are in tune, it is a good idea to double check by playing the higher notes (high A or high Bb).

<u>Tuning the Flute:</u>

Sharp = pull the head joint out

Flat = push the head joint in

In general, checking one note with a tuner will improve the intonation of the entire instrument. You don't need to check every single note with the tuner when you are just beginning. As you become more advanced, you'll become more aware of specific tendencies (i.e., high E tends to be sharp, whereas middle E tends to be flat). In general, though, tuning either A or Bb will ensure that your flute is properly tuned.

Basic Care for Your Flute

The flute is an expensive instrument, and you should care for it just as carefully as you care for your most prized possessions. Your flute will require regular cleaning after each practice session, but luckily this cleaning doesn't take long. Before you put your flute away in its case, you'll want to clean the head joint, body, and foot joint.

Most flutes come with a basic care kit, but if yours did not you will want to purchase a few items. For basic care, you will need either a cleaning rod plus a cleaning cloth, or some sort of swab. Most flutes come with a metal cleaning rod, but they are sometimes made out of wood as well. You will want to thread a corner of your cleaning cloth through the loop on the end of the cleaning rod.

Insert just a small portion of the cloth's corner until it is securely attached to the cleaning rod.

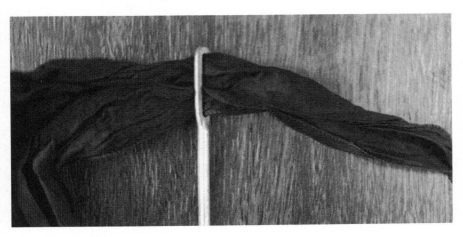

To clean the flute, you will insert this cleaning rod with the cloth attached into each different part of the instrument. To clean the body, you'll want to insert the cleaning rod all the way, and then twist it around a few times to ensure the cleaning cloth comes in contact with all sides of the body. Then you'll want to push one end of the cleaning rod further into the body in order to remove it. You will do the same with the foot joint, which will be much easier since it is not as long as the body. To clean the head joint, you'll want to push the cleaning rod and cloth into the head joint until it reaches the top. Twist the cleaning rod around a few times to ensure the cloth cleans all sides of the head joint, and then pull it out.

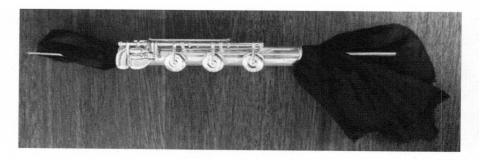

Many flutists also choose to polish their flute on a regular basis. If your flute did not come with a polishing cloth, they are readily available at most music stores. The polishing cloth is used to clean the surface of the flute - the keys and smooth areas. Be careful not to mess with any springs when polishing around the keys.

Chapter 3
Buying a Flute

Topics Covered

- Types of flutes

- Flute features

- Popular brands

- Choosing the right flute for you

Choosing to play the flute is an excellent choice. As you've begun to learn, the flute is an incredibly versatile instrument. You will be able to play your flute in nearly any setting you would like! Once you've made the decision to learn to play the flute, you will need to choose a flute to play. Selecting a flute is perhaps one of the most exciting parts of the process. The selection process may feel a bit overwhelming in the beginning, but this chapter will tell you everything you need to know to make the best choice.

Types of Flutes

When you are just starting to learn the flute, you will always learn on a concert flute. The **concert flute**, or C flute, is the most common type of flute. It is the flute seen in orchestras, bands, and ensemble performances throughout the world. Once you have mastered the C flute, there are a few different variations you may wish to explore. These different variations are most often seen in flute choir repertoire, or other small groups containing multiple flute parts.

Piccolo: The Piccolo is the most common variation of the flute to appear in the standard concert setting. One piccolo is usually present in all concert orchestras and bands. The Piccolo is almost an exact replica of the C flute, but is much smaller in size. The piccolo is able to play all of the same notes as the flute (with the exception of the lowest C), but the notes sound one octave higher in pitch. The Piccolo is well-known for its high, shrill sound. There is usually no more than one (or two at most) piccolo players in an ensemble, due to the nature of it's sound. Piccolos are sometimes made out of the same materials as a concert flute, but advanced level Piccolos are frequently made out of wood. The Piccolo is also in the key of C.

Alto Flute: The Alto Flute is another variation of the concert flute. It is considerably larger than the C flute, and is in the key of G. The alto flute's structure looks similar to a concert flute, but sometimes contains a curved head joint. This curved head joint allows the player to have easier access to the embouchure hole, without having to stretch the neck. There are still some versions of the alto flute with a straight head joint, looking the same as a concert flute. The Alto Flute sounds lower in pitch than the concert flute, but is played the same way. The structure of the Alto Flute is very similar to a concert flute, making the transition relatively easy for any flute player. The Alto Flute adds a warm, rich color to the sound of the ensemble, and is most frequently used in flute choirs — it rarely appears in concert bands or orchestras.

Bass Flute: The Bass Flute is the largest member of the flute family. It is significantly larger than the concert flute, and even larger than the Alto Flute. The Bass Flute sounds an entire octave lower than the concert flute, and is also in the key of C. The head joint of the Bass Flute is always curved in a J-shape to allow the player to access the embouchure hole. Most Bass Flutes are still played in a transverse manner, just like the concert flute. The Bass Flutes adds a darker sound to the ensemble, and again frequently appears in flute choir literature.

Flute Features

When selecting a flute to play, you will want to purchase (or rent) a Concert Flute. Concert Flutes are classified as either student, intermediate, or advanced/professional level flutes. Most C flutes contain the same basic structure and features, meaning that a student level flute is able to play the same music as an advanced level flute. However, there are a few minor differences which affect whether a flute is considered a student, intermediate or advanced model.

Open Hole vs. Closed Hole: The keys on the flute come in two varieties – open or closed hole. Closed hole keys (also known as Plateau-keys) and almost always used on student level flute. These keys are completely plated and covered, leaving no opening or area for air to escape.

Open hole keys (also known as French keys) have a small, circular opening in the middle of the key. These keys allow air to escape when the key is not being covered, providing a slightly more resonant sound. Open hole keys are often found on intermediate level flutes (though not always), and always found on professional models.

Intermediate flutes with open hole keys often come with small, clear plugs. These plugs can be placed inside the holes of the keys to completely cover them. Plugs are very useful during the transition to open hole keys, as they allow the player to take one plug out at a time while they adjust to the open holes.

Inline G vs. Offset G: Inline and offset G can both be found in all three classifications of flutes – student, intermediate and advanced. Inline and offset G describes the location of the "G" key on the flute (the key played with the ring finger of the left hand). This key is either "inline" – completely in line with the keys surrounding it, or "offset" – set out a little further than the other keys. An offset G is usually easier for beginners to play, as the structure of the key makes it a little easier for the player to reach with their ring finger. An inline G used to be common in more advanced flutes, but recently the offset G has gained popularity and is being seen in all different models of flutes. The choice of an inline G or offset G is entirely due to personal preference; there is no difference in sound.

This is an example of an offset G - the G key is set farther out than the other keys.

B Foot or C Foot: The foot joint of a concert flute varies in one major way — it is either a B foot or C foot. As discussed in the previous chapter, a C foot joint contains only two circular keys. The C foot joint allows the player to play down to low C. It contains just one roller key and is almost always the model used in student level flutes. The B foot joint extends the range a half step lower, to low B. This foot joint contains three circular keys and two roller keys. Most intermediate and professional level flutes have a B foot joint. A low B is not written in most beginner level music, so the B foot is usually not needed until a player becomes more advanced.

Split E: The split E is a mechanism added to the flute to allow for extra venting when the musician plays a high E. This note is a challenging note on the flute, so the split E makes it a little easier for this note to come out. It is a simple piece of metal that appears near the Ab key and looks like a small rod between the keys. This mechanism vents the G key, which makes playing a high E much easier and more attainable. The split E mechanism is most commonly seen in flutes with an offset G, but can sometimes be added to a flute with an inline G. It can be found on some student level flutes and is usually found in all intermediate and advanced flute structures (those with an offset G).

Split E mechanism

C# Trill: The C# trill is an additional lever found in the middle of the body of the flute, which assists in trilling from B to C#. It can be used for multiple other trill fingerings but is not necessary. This is an additional feature sometimes found on intermediate and advanced level flutes, but not always. A flute with a second lever in the middle of the body contains a C# trill key.

Silver Plated: Most student level flutes are made out of metals like nickel and alloy. Once you begin to search for more advanced flutes, you will usually find an option to purchase a silver-plated flute. Silver plating is thought to increase the resonance of the flute and give it a richer sound. Silver plating (or solid silver) is often considerably more expensive, but for players hoping to grow with their instrument, silver plating is a great quality to consider.

Popular Flute Brands

Altus: The Altus flute company is based out of Azumino, Japan. Their flutes are created for a "growing player", meaning that they are suitable for beginner flutists but still provide room for growth and improvement. The Azumi models are a great compromise for beginners looking for a long-term flute that is still affordable. These flutes are best suited for serious beginner or intermediate students hoping to grow and continue.

Armstrong: Armstrong was founded by an instrument repairman, who opened his first company in Elkhart, Indiana. Armstrong builds a sturdy beginner level flute, but is usually not the most beneficial for intermediate or advanced players. The head joints on these flutes are known to be a little harder to blow, so once players begin to refine their embouchure and tone, it is more challenging to advance on this type of head joint. Armstrong flutes are best suited for beginner players.

Gemeinhardt: The Gemeinhardt company was founded by a flute maker who later acquired a piccolo company as well. The makers of these flutes use softer metals to create the instrument, therefore the keys and rods more susceptible to moving and bending. Gemeinhardt is a popular beginner level flute that is quite affordable, but often limits abilities for intermediate and advanced players.

Jupiter: Jupiter Band Instruments, Inc. was originally founded in Taiwan, and has since created a US base in Austin, Texas. Their company slogan is "a world of quality goes into each musical instrument", which guides their production. This slogan seems to have proven to be true, as their flutes continue to rank in the top seller lists. Jupiter flutes are a great choice for intermediate and advanced level flutists.

Muramatsu: Muramatsu flutes have been available for sale in the United States since 1975. Muramatsu is known for their professional level flutes, and claims to sell more professional flutes worldwide than any other company. Their unique craftmanship provides these flutes a dark, distinguished tone. These flutes are an excellent choice for musicians making the leap to a professional level flute.

Pearl: The Pearl Music Company was originally founded in Japan, but has since created a US base in Nashville, Tennessee to create a line of flutes. Pearl flutes are known to be dependable, and are available in student, intermediate and advanced models.

Yamaha: The Yamaha Corp. is based in Japan, and first began their company selling reed organs. In 1960, they began selling various instruments. Yamaha flutes have consistently ranked well among flute players of all ability levels. The Yamaha series of flutes provides different models for different ability levels. These flutes are known to be dependable and are very affordable for their quality. Yamaha flutes suit students from beginner levels all the way to advanced.

Choosing the Right Flute for You

These companies, along with the many others available, provide a wide range flutes to choose from. Selecting a flute may feel overwhelming at first, but it is worth spending some time on this decision. Ultimately, selecting a flute comes down to personal preference. Each individual has unique characteristics that may make them well suited for certain types of flutes and unsuited for others.

The biggest piece of advice to remember when selecting a flute is that you should play the instrument yourself before purchasing, or at least have a professional whom you trust test it out. Purchasing a flute online without trying it first can be a risky decision. It is best to talk to a music or flute professional when narrowing down your options. Beginner level flutes can often be purchased used. For a student who is unsure how long they plan to continue studying the flute, this can be a great option. Here are a few things to consider when selecting your flute.

What is your price range? You can often find a used, student level flute for as little as $100 - $500 dollars. Depending on the wear and tear, these flutes can be a great place to start. (Just make sure you play the flute BEFORE purchasing it!). New student flutes usually cost less than $1,000, with prices varying depending on the model. Intermediate flutes range anywhere from $500 - $3,000, while professional flutes often cost anything from $3,000 upwards.

What brand of flutes fall within your price range? As you can see, flute prices fluctuate dramatically depending on the maker and type of flute. Once you set a price range, you can determine what makers sell flutes that fall within this price range. If you don't know, ask!

How long are you planning on playing the flute? If you plan to play the flute for many years, a flute that will give you room to grow is your best bet. If you are still unsure how long you will continue, you may want to try a student flute first before making a significant investment. If you plan to advance very quickly, perhaps you could look into intermediate models that come with plugs for their open holes.

What specific characteristics are you looking for? Do you know for sure that you want an offset G? Use this to narrow down your search. If you want closed hole keys for your first flute, write this down as well.

Try multiple different flutes before purchasing one. You never truly know what you like and dislike until you've had the opportunity to try a wide variety. Head to your local music store and ask to try flutes (its okay to try 5 or 6 at a time)! The music store representative will be very helpful in assisting you as you narrow down your search. If you are ordering online, you can always order a few and return the ones you don't like (assuming you check the return policy ahead of time). Take your time - you will know the right flute when you find it.

Resources

- Flute World: https://www.fluteworld.com

- Woodwind Brasswind: https://www.wwbw.com/

- Guitar Center: https://www.guitarcenter.com/Flutes-Piccolos

Chapter 4
Understanding Music Notes & Rhythm

Topics Covered

- Understanding the staff

- Reading note names

- Flats and sharps

- Key signatures and time signatures

- Counting basic rhythms

Now that you've selected your flute, the fun part begins. Playing the flute is the most exciting part of this journey – so in order to get there, you first need to understand a bit of the music basics. This chapter will teach you everything you need to know to read your very first music book and start playing flute music.

Understanding the Staff

In order to read music, you'll need to know a few basic things about where music notes are placed. All music is read on what is called a staff. This staff consists of 5 lines and 4 spaces. Music notes fall somewhere within these lines and spaces, or above and below the staff using extra lines and spaces. Below is an example of the musical staff.

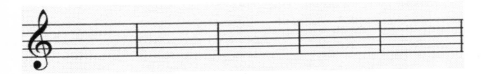

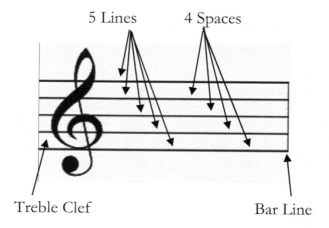

Flute music is all written in **Treble Clef**, which is the S shaped symbol that appears at the beginning of each line of music. The clef designates how we will identify note names. Since all flute music is written in treble clef, that is how we are going to learn note names. A **Bar Line** appears at the end of each measure of music. The length of a measure is designated by the time signature (which we will learn below). The important thing to remember about these bar lines is that their purpose is simply to divide the music up into sections - they are not a note or rhythm that needs to be played. You can simply skip over them when reading music.

Reading Note Names

Lucky for you, the flute sounds in the key of C, meaning that each note you play sounds exactly as written. Instruments that are not in the key of C sound a different note than what they play, which means that they often have to transpose. The flute will never have to transpose when playing concert music, which makes reading music much simpler.

Learning the note names is an important step in beginning to play the flute. Once you have mastered the note names, you will be able to look at a piece of music and know which note to play on your flute. The most common way to learn note names is through the use of mnemonic devices. When the notes are arranged in a certain order, you can spell a word or think of a phrase to help you remember their order.

The letter names for notes in each of the four spaces on the staff, starting with the lowest space, spell the word FACE.

F   A   C   E

The letter names for notes on each of the five lines on the staff, starting with the lowest line, are EGBDF. Phrases are often used to remember the order of these letters, such as Every Good Boy Deserves Fudge, or Every Good Boy Does Fine.

Every **G**ood **B**oy **D**eserves **F**udge

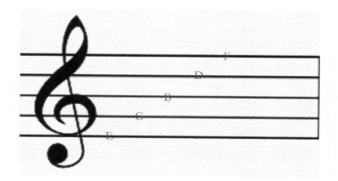

Flats and Sharps

Flats and sharps, otherwise known as accidentals, are symbols that appear next to a note to either lower or raise its pitch one half step. When you see a flat or sharp next to a note, be aware that it is played with a different fingering on your flute. For example, a regular B has one fingering, where as a B flat has another. A flat sign looks like a lowercase B: b, and a sharp sign looks like the number symbol: #. In a band setting, flutes typically find themselves playing flats, whereas in an orchestra setting, flutes will often play sharps. To write out the letter names of a note that is flat (B flat, for example) you write the symbol *after* the letter: Bb. To write out F sharp, you would write F#. In the music, the flats and sharps always appear directly *in front* of the note.

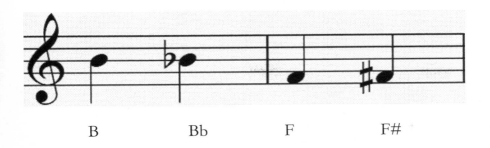

| B | Bb | F | F# |

Key Signatures and Time Signatures

Another place that flats and sharps can be found is in what's called the **key signature**. At the beginning of a piece of music, flats and sharps often appear immediately after the treble clef. These accidentals appear either in a space or on a line, and designate that note to be flat/sharp throughout the entire song.

For example:

This key signature contains two flats. To determine the notes that are flat, you will need to use EGBDF (Every Good Boy Deserves Fudge) if the flat is on a line, and FACE if the flat is in a space.

The first flat in this key signature appears on a line – the third line from the bottom. Using the saying "every good boy deserves fudge", we can determine that the third letter (Boy) is a B. Therefore, all of the B's we see in this song will be flat: Bb.

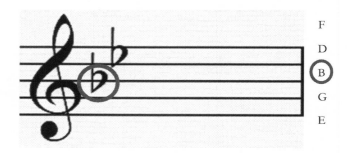

The second flat in this key signature appears in a space – the fourth space from the bottom. Using the word FACE, we can determine that the fourth space is the letter E. Therefore, all E's we see in this song will also be flat: Eb.

The key signature will vary greatly once you begin to read more challenging music, but the most common key signature you will find in beginning flute music is the one seen above, containing Bb and Eb.

Another notation you will see at the beginning of a piece of music is the **time signature**. As mentioned before, the time signature determines how many beats fall into each measure, and what type of note gets a beat. The time signature looks like a fraction, with one number above another.

The time signature appears directly after the key signature in a piece of music. It will look something like this:

This time signature is called 4/4 (read: four four), otherwise known as common time. The top number tells us how many notes are in a measure (in this case, 4 notes) and the bottom note tells us what note gets the beat. To figure out what type of note gets the beat, replace the top number with a one and read the time signature as if it were a fraction. For example, ¼ is also known as a quarter. This means that the quarter note gets the beat. Now we know that a quarter note will receive one beat, and 4 quarter notes make up a measure. At the end of every measure you will find a bar line.

This is the most common key signature (4/4) you will find - hence its name, common time - especially in beginning flute music. Now that we understand the basic symbols and letter names, it's time to put them in action with some rhythm.

Counting Basic Rhythms

The most basic skill you will utilize to understand rhythm is the ability to keep a steady beat. When you listen to a piece of music and find yourself tapping your toe, clapping along, or swaying to the music, you are moving to the beat of the music. The ability to "feel" a piece of music means that you are able to identify the pulse of the music. We use this sense of pulse when counting any type of rhythm – anything from basic to advanced.

This section will discuss the basic rhythms you will find in any flute music. Understanding these rhythms will allow you to play a wide variety of music on your flute. These rhythms are found in every type of music – no matter its difficulty, style, or instrumentation. These rhythms provide the foundation which you will use throughout the rest of your musical career. Let's get started on some basic music notes and rests.

The four types of note rhythms we will learn are as follows:

Whole Note   Half Note   Quarter Note   Eighth Notes

When reading rhythms, we first begin by learning to count each beat using a number. Each beat receives one number, and we continue counting until we reach the end of the measure (shown by a bar line). For example, in common time, the top number of the key signature is 4. This means that there are 4 beats (counts) in each measure. We will count 1-2-3-4, and then start over once we reach 4: 1-2-3-4, 1-2-3-4, etc. In this time signature, a quarter note receives the beat, which means that a **quarter note receives one count.**

1 2 3 4   1 2 3 4   1 2 3 4

This number tells us that there are 4 beats in a measure, meaning we count up to 4 and then start over.

A **half note receives two beats,** or two counts. A half note is identified by the fact that it is an open note (not colored black), and has a stem attached to it.

1-2   3-4   1-2   3-4   1-2   3-4

A **whole note receives four beats,** or four counts. A whole note is identified by the fact that it is an open note (not colored in black), and has no stem. A whole note looks like an oval on the staff.

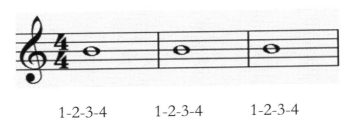

1-2-3-4   1-2-3-4   1-2-3-4

These three basic rhythms make up most beginning flute songs. Once you get into more intermediate music, you may find some eighth notes written in your songs. Eighth notes are unlike quarter notes, half notes, and whole notes because **one eighth note receives only half a beat**. This means that two eighth notes fit into one beat – they are played twice as fast as a quarter note.

When counting eighth notes, the first eighth note always receives the beat (or the number). The second eighth note is counted by saying "and" (&). A full measure of eighth notes would be counted 1-&-2-&-3-&-4-&. Eighth notes look very similar to quarter notes in the fact that they are colored in black and contain a stem. What makes them different is that an eighth note has a flag attached to their stem.

Eighth Note Quarter Note Two eighth notes together
(has a flag on the stem) (no flag on the stem)(two eighth notes make up one beat)

When taking up a full measure, eighth notes would be counted as follows:

1 & 2 & 3 & 4 & 1 & 2 & 3 & 4 &

Whole Note = 4 Beats

Half Note = 2 Beats

Quarter Note = 1 Beat

Eighth Note = ½ Beat

Similarly, there are also rests in music that correspond to each of these notes. A **rest** means that there is silence – no sound or music is played during a rest. We will discuss three basic types of rests in this chapter: a whole rest, half rest and quarter rest.

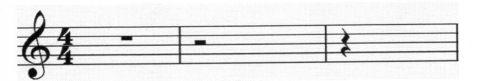

Whole Rest   Half Rest   Quarter Rest

Each of these rests receive the same number of beats as the corresponding note. For example, a **whole** rest receives 4 beats, just as a **whole** note receive 4 beats.

Whole Rest = 4 Beats

Half Rest = 2 Beats

Quarter Rest = 1 Beat

You may notice that the whole rest and half rest look very similar. The difference between the whole and half rest lies in the position in which they are found on the staff. A whole rest hangs below the line, where as a half rests sits above the line. A common way to remember this is that a whole rest is "in the hole", while a half rest "looks like a hat".

Rests are counted numerically, just as the notes were counted above.

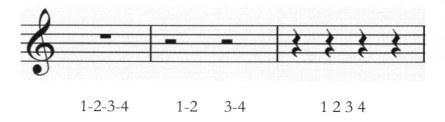

1-2-3-4   1-2   3-4   1 2 3 4

There are also eighth rests, which receive half of a beat, but we will not get into those in this chapter. Eighth rests are usually not found in beginner flute music, as they are more of an intermediate technique.

While learning basic rhythm counting for the first time may feel very overwhelming, it makes a lot more sense when put in context. Once you begin reading music and playing your first songs, these rhythms will start to feel very familiar. After a little bit of practice, you will be counting many different rhythms without even stopping to think about it.

Chapter 5
How to Play Notes on the Flute

Topics Covered

- Proper posture and breathing

- Flute embouchure

- How to hold the flute

- Notes and fingerings on the flute

- Tonguing and articulation

Now that you have a basic understanding of note names and rhythms, you are ready to begin playing your flute! All of the music theory that you just learned will now come into context as you begin playing different notes. This chapter will teach you what you need to know to breathe properly, make a sound on your flute, and play different notes.

Proper Posture and Breathing

Playing any wind instrument requires a great deal of air and breath support. To do this, you'll need to make sure you are playing with proper posture. If your upper body is hunched over, your lungs and diaphragm will not be able to fully expand, thus limiting your air supply and diminishing the quality of your sound.

To avoid this, it's best to learn proper posture before you even begin playing the flute. You can choose to either sit or stand while you play your flute. If you choose to stand, your upper body is prevented from slouching as dramatically as when you are sitting, thus eliminating most of the poor posture issues you may encounter in a chair. If you choose to play the flute while sitting, you will need to be especially aware of your posture.

You should begin by sitting on the very front edge of your chair, with your back away from the back of the chair. Plant your feet firmly on the floor in front of you. Sit up tall, so you back is fully straightened. A good way to test this is to stand up once you have positioned your feet, and then sit back down. Your upper body should remain in the exact same position when you sit back down as it was when you were standing. Keep your shoulders back, allowing plenty of room for your chest and diaphragm to expand.

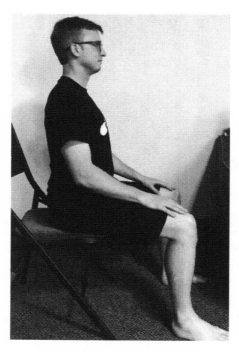

Contrary to our intuition, deep breathing is completed by expanding the diaphragm, not the lungs. When you inhale deeply, focus on expanding your diaphragm, which is located beneath your ribs, right around your stomach. Your shoulders should never rise when you take a deep breath. Take a deep breath and practice expanding your stomach as far as you can. Practice breathing in slowly, until your diaphragm is completely full.

A great breathing exercise is to practice breathing in and out at different speeds. To practice this, begin by inhaling for 4 counts, and then exhaling for 4 counts. Immediately after exhaling, inhale for 6 counts and then exhale for 6. Transition immediately to inhale for 8, then exhale for 8. Next, inhale for 10, exhale for 10. Finally, inhale for 12, exhale for 12. This exercise should be completed with no breaks in between, so you are continuously inhaling or exhaling. The goal of the exercise is to completely fill your diaphragm with air by the end of your inhale – you will need to take in air faster when you only have 4 counts, and much slower when you inhale for 12. You will have the same goal on the exhale – you should completely empty your air by the end of the exhalation period.

Spending time on the fundamentals is not necessarily the most exciting exercise, but it will pay off big time by the time you play your flute. Having solid fundamentals in place will allow you to progress much quicker on your instrument.

Flute Embouchure

Once your posture is in place and you have practiced a few breathing exercises, you are ready to make your first sounds on the flute. As we mentioned in the first few chapters, the flute is unlike other instruments in the way that it produces sound. You will never place your mouth or lips completely over the embouchure hole, unlike other wind instruments.

To begin practicing your embouchure, you will want to start by using just the flute head joint. The head joint is the part of the flute that produces sound. Practicing on the head joint alone provides you time to establish a really strong sound with the least amount of resistance. Practice creating a sound on just the head joint a few times before adding the rest of the flute.

Before you begin playing, you will always want to check your posture. Check that you are sitting on the front edge of the chair, with your back straight and feet planted firmly on the floor. Bring the head joint up to your bottom lip. You will want the open end to be pointed to the right, with the top of the head joint to your left.

Closed end on your left   Open end on your right

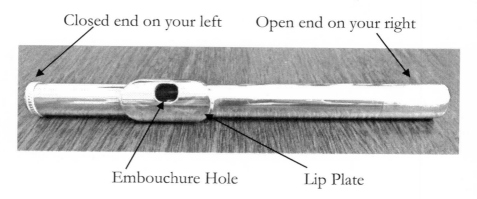

Embouchure Hole   Lip Plate

Place your lower lip on the lip plate, centering it to the embouchure hole. You will want approximately 1/3 of your lip to cover the opening of the hole.

To play the flute, you will need to blow air across this embouchure hole, directing the air down towards the instrument. Creating a sound on the flute is very similar to blowing over the top of a pop bottle. You may need to adjust the head joint slightly to create a sound for the first time. If you are unable to make a sound right away, experiment by rolling the head joint slightly in or out, or move your lower lip to cover slightly more or less of the embouchure hole.

You will need to use a very steady air stream in order to create enough resistance to make a sound. Simply exhaling will not be enough. Using your abdomen, strongly exhale, keeping the air moving for more than just a few counts (much like you did during the breathing exercise). It may take a bit of experimentation to find the set up that works for you, but once you create your first sound you will no doubt be able to recreate it much quicker.

Listening Example #2: Makin a Sound on the Head Joint

https://soundcloud.com/jason_randall/sets/how-to-play-the-flute

When you practice playing just the head joint, the sound may surprise you. Notice how the sound produced by just the head joint is quite different than the sound of a full flute.

How to Hold the Flute

Once you feel comfortable making a sound on the head joint, you are ready to attach the body and foot joint. Put your flute together as discussed in the beginning chapters of this book. Make sure to align your embouchure hole with the very first key on the body, and to center the rod on the foot joint with the last key of the body.

The body of the flute is held on your right side. Bring the embouchure hole on the head joint up to lower lip, exactly as you did when you played only the head joint. Your right hand will hold the flute on the lower end of the body. Place your pinky on the very first key of the foot joint, closest to the body of the flute. Place your ring finger on the last key of the body, middle finger directly to its left, and index finger directly to the left of your middle finger.

Place your right thumb on the body of the flute underneath the index finger, and adjust your wrist so this finger placement feels comfortable.

Pinky   Ring Finger

(first key of the foot joint)   (last key on the body)

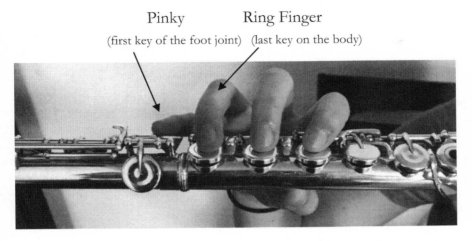

Extend your left arm directly out in front of you, and reach around the flute to place your left fingers on the keys. Your ring finger will be placed on the key nearest to your Ab key. Place your middle finger directly to its left, and index finger to the left of your middle finger (skip one key in between).

Ab Key   Ring Finger

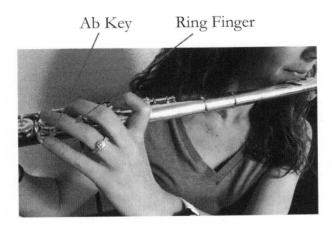

Place your left thumb on the lever on the back side of the body.

You should aim to hold your flute so it is parallel to the floor. This may be tricky in the beginning, as the flute feels very heavy and long compared to just the head joint. Practice placing your fingers in the proper position and then lifting them off the keys. When your fingers are not pushing down a key, they should remain directly above the key in a curved, relaxed position. This allows you easy access to those keys once you begin to play different notes.

Notes and Fingerings

The flute has the ability to play every single note in a chromatic scale. As mentioned before, a regular B has a different fingering than a Bb. We are going to learn the finger positions for the notes in a Bb scale, which is the most common key signature in beginner flute music. This scale covers a wide range of notes, but even so, once you get more advanced you may wish to play music that involves notes that are outside of this scale. When you get to this point, you can find many flute fingering charts for free online or in the back of your music book. A great thing about the flute is that most notes with the same name (for example, low **Bb** and high **Bb**) are fingered the same way, even if they are in different octaves.

We are first going to learn the notes in a Bb scale. The Bb scale looks like this:

Bb   C   D   Eb   F   G   A   Bb

It may also look slightly different if there is a key signature. This key signature tells us that both B and E are flat, so we don't need to see the flat signs next to the notes. The scale below consists of the same notes and same finger positions as above.

Bb   C   D   Eb   F   G   A   Bb

You can determine the note names in this example by using the same techniques we discussed in the note and rhythm chapter. Use the word FACE to help you find letter names in the spaces, and EGBDF (Every Good Boy Deserves Fudge) to help you determine letter names of notes on the lines. Remember that we always start from the bottom space or line when using these sayings/phrases.

You may notice that the last three notes in this scale are placed above the staff. We use what is called ledger lines to differentiate between these notes. Ledger lines are the small lines that you see in the middle of or below these notes. As you begin playing your flute, you will want to memorize these three notes and their position above the staff.

Ledger Lines

As mentioned before, each of these notes are played using a different finger placement. The diagram below represents your finger placement on the keys of the flute. When a circle is colored black, you will push down that key. If the circle is open, you will leave your finger off the key.

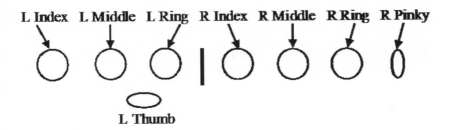

Let's learn the finger placements for the scale in order, beginning with our Bb on the middle line of the staff.

Bb Scale Fingering Chart

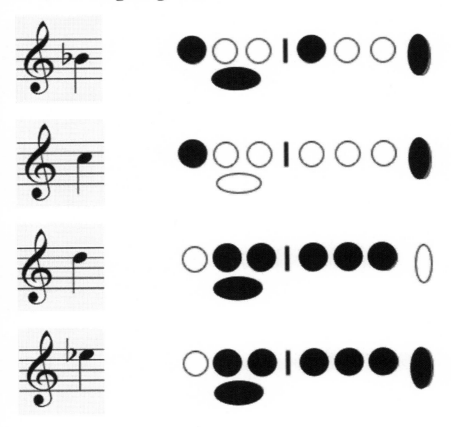

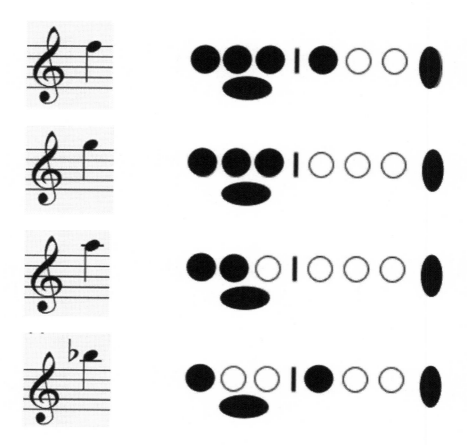

It's important to note that the low Bb and high Bb are played using the same finger position. This makes it a lot easier to remember the fingerings for each of these notes, but it means that you will need to make a few changes to your embouchure in order to get the correct sound.

Listening Example #3: The Bb Scale

https://soundcloud.com/jason_randall/sets/how-to-play-the-flute

In track 3, listen to the Bb scale as it is played in whole notes, half notes, quarter notes and eighth notes. All major scales follow the same pattern, and will sound very similar when played correctly.

Differentiating between low and high notes is all completed through the strength of your air stream and direction of the air. To create low notes, you will want to use a slightly slower, more relaxed air stream. To create high notes, you'll need to use a faster, stronger air stream. Aim the air downwards into the flute using fast air. Higher notes are often harder for beginners to play because they require a faster air stream.

A great way to get the feel for the air pressure you are using is to practice the breathing exercise mentioned earlier in this chapter, but exhale by hissing, rather than just blowing out air. The hiss will allow you to hear the difference between faster and slower air. When you exhale all of your air in shorter periods of time (i.e., at the beginning of the breathing exercise when you exhale for only 4 or 6 counts) you should hear a louder hiss. This is the type of air you will want to use to produce high notes. When you have more time to expend all of your air (i.e., at the end of the breathing exercise when you exhale for 10 or 12 counts) you will hear a softer, less forceful hiss. This is the type of air you will want to use to produce low notes.

Being able to properly control your air stream will take time and lots of practice. Practicing long tones is a great way to develop better control of your sound on the flute. Practice playing each of the notes in your Bb scale as whole notes. Hold each note out for 4 full counts, and see if you can create a consistent sound during that time.

Tonguing and Articulation

When you play any note, you will want it to start with a clear, crisp sound (unless otherwise notated in the music). To achieve this, you will want to start each of the notes with your tongue, a technique we call tonguing. Tonguing is a type of **articulation**. Articulation encompasses many different techniques that designate the attack, strength, and length of notes.

Once you begin to play notes and music on your flute, you will want to get in the habit of tonguing every single note. To tongue a note, you will need to start the note by touching the tip of your tongue to the back of your top front teeth. You can practice how this feels by simply saying "to-to-to-to-to". The placement of your tongue at the beginning of each "to" is where you will want it to be located to tongue each note. Next, practice saying "to", but extend the word so it is really long and drawn out: "tooooo-toooooo". The T in this word represents tonguing the beginning of each note, and the ooooo represents the air you will use to play this note on your flute.

To practice tonguing on the flute, first start by playing whole notes. Find a note that you feel comfortable playing, and practice starting the note with your tongue each time. Once you feel more comfortable with this technique, practice playing half notes and then quarter notes while tonguing each note.

Many beginner flute players mistakenly think they are tonguing the note when they begin the sound using only their air. This gives them more of a "who" sound that is unclear and less defined. You will be able to tell if you are doing this by paying attention to your tongue placement while you play. Does it stay in one spot? Or are you moving it from the top of your mouth, behind your front teeth after each note? If your tongue is not moving, you are most likely not tonguing the notes.

Tonguing may feel very foreign as you first begin to play your flute. It feels unnatural to move your tongue around as if you were speaking while blowing air into your flute. Just like any other flute technique, this will get easier and feel more comfortable with time. Practicing these basic techniques is what will allow you to build a strong foundation, and help you play full songs with ease.

Listening Example #4: Tonguing Techniques

https://soundcloud.com/jason_randall/sets/how-to-play-the-flute

In track 4, first listen to notes played on the flute without tonguing, and then listen to the difference of notes played *with* tonguing. Next, listen to an exercise you can use to practice tonguing with a whole note – half note – quarter note progression.

Chapter 6
Playing Your First Song

Topics Covered

- Flute warm ups

- Scale studies

- Musical Examples

You are ready to start playing some songs on your flute! Now that you've learned different notes, rhythms, finger placements, and how to make a sound, let's get to work playing your first song. This chapter will teach you some basic warm ups to play at the beginning of every practice session, more scales to improve your technical abilities, and a few different songs to get started playing.

Flute Warm Ups

Warming up is an essential portion of any practice session. Whether you are a beginner or professional musician, warming up should be the first thing you do each time you play your flute. Warming up not only gets air flowing through the instrument, but it allows your fingers and facial muscles to get ready to work hard. Warm ups on wind instrument usually consist of long tones or some slower, easier melodies. These warm ups also usually involve some scales and technical exercises.

While there are no specific exercises you need to play for your warm up, there are a few guidelines you should follow when deciding what to play to warm up. A few guidelines to follow when selecting a warm up:

- Include some long tones, or songs with long notes (such as whole notes)

- Begin with lower notes before working your way up to high notes

- Get in the habit of regularly practicing scales

Here are a few examples of potential warm ups you could include in your practice session. Your warm up does not need to take long (just a few minutes), but should always be the first thing you play before diving in to your music. Play through each of these exercises at a slow, steady speed to get warmed up before playing your songs. Practice sustaining the sound throughout each measure, and do not rush.

Long Tone Exercise #1

Long Tone Exercise #2

Long Tone Exercise #3

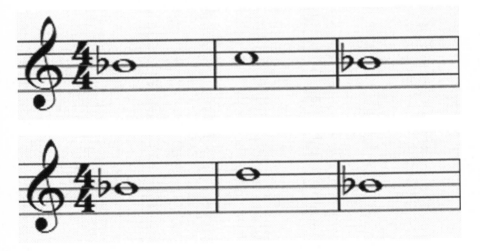

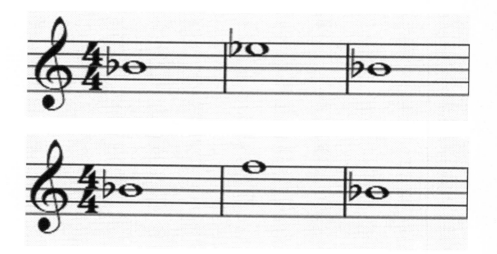

Listening Example #5: Long Tone Exercises

https://soundcloud.com/jason_randall/sets/how-to-play-the-flute

In track 5, listen to long tone exercises 1, 2 and 3.

Scale Studies

Scales are important exercises for any musician. You should get in the habit of regularly playing through one or two scales each time you practice. Scales help you become familiar with different key signatures and different combinations of notes, which will eventually improve your site reading and technical skills on the flute. Learning the Bb scale first (the scale from the previous chapter) is a great place to start.

Once you become familiar with all of these notes and can play them with a strong confident sound, you can begin to learn other scales. The best scales to begin with are the Bb, F, and Eb major scales. For your reference, here are all of the major scales you can learn on the flute.

C Major Scale

F Major Scale

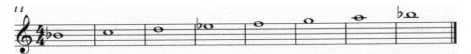

Bb Major Scale

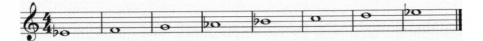

Eb Major Scale

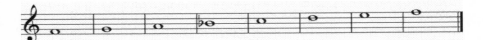

Ab Major Scale

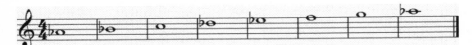

Db Major Scale

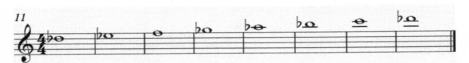

Gb Major Scale

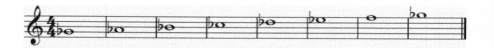

Listening Example #6: 7 Major Scales

https://soundcloud.com/jason_randall/sets/how-to-play-the-flute

In track 6, listen to all 7 major scales played using quarter notes. The scales are played in order of the circle of 5ths (the order they appear above).

Begin practicing your Bb scale each time you play your flute. You can play your scale in whole notes, half notes, quarter notes, or any other rhythm you would like. Practice going up and then coming back down – starting from the highest note and working your way back down to the lowest note.

It's important to get really familiar with one scale before moving on to the next or adding another. All major scales have the same pattern and sound, so practicing one scale until you can play it confidently will help train your ear to learn the sounds of a major scale. Once you can confidently play the Bb scale, you can begin learning another scale – the F major or Eb major scales are a great next step. Learn you scales thoroughly, one at a time, and practice them with multiple different rhythms each time.

Musical Examples

After spending a few minutes playing long tones and a scale exercise, you are ready to dive into some songs! The possibilities of what you can learn on your flute are endless. Beginning flute music typically includes just a few notes at one time, and the basic rhythms that we learned in the previous chapter. If you come across any notes that you do not know, remember to use the saying Every Good Boy Deserves Fudge if the note is on a line, and FACE if the note is on a space. I would highly suggest downloading a free flute fingering chart that will tell you how to play any note on the flute. If you purchased a book of flute music, there are often fingering charts right in the beginning or end page of the book.

It's time to get started playing music! Here are a few songs you can begin to play on your flute.

Hot Cross Buns

<u>Listening Example #7: Hot Cross Buns</u>

<u>https://soundcloud.com/jason_randall/sets/how-to-play-the-flute</u>

Twinkle Twinkle Little Star

In the excerpt above, you may notice that not all of the B's have a flat sign next to them. For example, if you look in the very first measure, the first two notes are both a B. The first note has a flat sign in front of it, but the second does not. However, both of these notes are still Bb. In music, if you see an accidental (flat, sharp, or natural) next to a note, **the accidental carries through the measure**. If there is another note that is the same letter name before the bar line, that note will also be affected by the accidental.

Since the very first B in this measure has a flat sign next to it, any other B that appears in this measure will also be a Bb, even if there is no flat sign by it. This remains true in measure 3 of the song, when the first E has a flat in front of it but the second does not – both of these notes are still Eb.

Listening Example #8: Twinkle Twinkle Little Star

https://soundcloud.com/jason_randall/sets/how-to-play-the-flute

Yankee Doodle

There are a few notes in Yankee Doodle that do not appear in the Bb scale. For example, the last note in measure 2 is in the very bottom space. Using FACE, we can determine that this note is a F (the first space). Use FACE and EGBDF to determine the note names for any new notes you find in this song.

All of the low notes have the same fingering as the high notes. For example, this low F in Yankee Doodle has the same finger placement as the F found in your Bb scale.

Listening Example #9: Yankee Doodle

https://soundcloud.com/jason_randall/sets/how-to-play-the-flute

Ode to Joy

Listening Example #10: Ode to Joy

https://soundcloud.com/jason_randall/sets/how-to-play-the-flute

Music for many beginning flute songs can be downloaded online for free. Check out the resources page at the end of this book for different websites from which you can download more songs. These four songs are only the beginning! Once you get started making music on your flute, the possibilities are endless.

Chapter 7
Intermediate Flute Techniques

Topics Covered

- Articulation

- Dynamics

- Vibrato

- Trills

Now that you've played a few songs on your flute and gotten a bit more confident with your sound, it's time to learn a few intermediate techniques. Once you have been practicing for a bit, you may want to learn some more challenging music. When you find more difficult music, there are a few markings and techniques that you will need to know in order to play this music. In this chapter, you will learn more advanced musical notation as well as a few more advanced techniques to begin practicing on your flute.

Articulation

When you first learned to make sounds on the flute, you learned about the importance of tonguing. If you remember back from earlier in the book, we discussed that tonguing was a type of articulation. "Articulation encompasses many different techniques that designate the attack, strength, and length of notes." Beginning each of the notes with your tongue separates each note from the next, giving it a clear attack and precise sound.

While you will need to tongue (or "articulate") each note in most songs, there are a few instances where you will *not* want to tongue the notes. One of them is when you see a **slur**. A slur is curved marking in your music that appears above or below multiple notes.

When you see a slur in your music, it means that you will not tongue the notes underneath it. You will articulate the very first note and continue your air as you move your fingers. Do not stop your air in between each note or separate the notes in any way. A slur indicates that this particular section of the music should sound as smooth as possible, with no breaks in the sound for the duration of the slur.

Listening Example #11: Slur Excerpt

https://soundcloud.com/jason_randall/sets/how-to-play-the-flute

In track 11, the exercise above is played first without a slur (tonguing all notes) and then as written, with the slur. Notice the difference between tonguing and slurring.

Another marking that looks very similar to a slur is called a **tie**. A tie also appears as a curved marking above or below notes - the difference is that a tie appears above two or more notes that are the same. The tie indicates that only the first note should be articulated, and your air should continue without separating the notes. Since the notes are the same, it will sound like one long note. In the example below you will articulate the beginning of your half note, and hold the D all the way through beat one of the next measure.

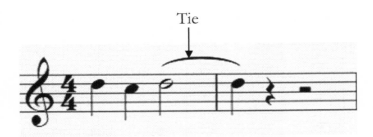

You can differentiate between ties and slurs only by the notes that are underneath the marking. For example:

Another articulation marking you may find in intermediate flute music is a **tenuto**. A tenuto looks like a small horizontal line on top of or below a note. This tenuto indicates that you should play the note for its full length, and very smoothly. When you see a tenuto marking it is designating that the note or notes in which they appear should be played very smoothly, with a legato style.

When you see a tenuto mark, you will still need to tongue the note, but it should begin very delicately with a soft attack. There should be a distinct start to the note, but little separation and space. Hold the note(s) out for its full length to ensure there is no break or gap in the sound between notes.

Tenuto

In contrast, another articulation marking you may see is a **staccato**. A staccato mark is a small dot that appears above or below a note. The staccato indicates that you should play each note very short and separated. Tonguing is very important in sections of music where staccatos appear. You will want the beginning of each note to sound very clear, with a hard attack. The note length will be very short – just long enough to get out sound and establish a pitch. There should be space heard between each note in a staccato section.

Staccato

One final articulation marking that you may find in intermediate music is an **accent**. Accents are a combination of articulation technique and dynamic. Accents are most commonly found in marches, or strong, emphasized sections of other music. An accent looks like a "greater-than" symbol above or below a note (>). It indicates that the note should be brought out and emphasized. To do so, you will need to play accented notes louder, with a strong attack and space in between each note.

Tonging is incredibly important for accented notes; you will need a very strong, hard attack with your tongue. The beginning of each accented note should be very clear and emphasized. Accents are used to bring out a certain note or section in the music. Always remember to maintain a controlled sound when playing accented notes – do not overblow or blow so hard that your tone suffers.

Accent

These five styles of articulation allow you to play a wide variety of music. Adding in different types of articulation really brings a piece of music to life. Through the use of articulation, you can differentiate between multiple sections of the music, give them each meaning, and begin to play with musicality.

<u>Listening Example #12: Tenuto, Staccato, and Accent</u>

https://soundcloud.com/jason_randall/sets/how-to-play-the-flute

In track 12, you will hear the exercise above played three different times.
The first time, the exercise is played using tenutos.
The second time, the exercise is played using staccatos.
And the third time, the exercise is played using accents.

Articulations

- Slur or Tie = Smooth, Connected Notes

- Tenuto = Long Notes, Soft Attack

- Staccato = Short, Crisp Notes

- Accent = Emphasized Notes, Strong Attack

Dynamics

Another musical technique you will find in intermediate flute music is the use of dynamics. The word **dynamic** is a musical term that refers to the volume at which the music is performed. There are many different types of dynamics, much like articulations. Some dynamics tell you what volume to play an entire section, while others tell you what volume to play a single note. Some dynamic markings indicate that your volume should gradually increase or decrease. Here are a few dynamic markings to know.

Loud dynamic levels: **forte and mezzo forte**. In music, the most common dynamic markings you will see indicate that a section should be played at either a loud or soft level. When a section is meant to be played with a strong, confident sound it will be marked with either a forte or mezzo forte. These dynamics are abbreviated f and mf in music. Forte is an Italian word for loud, meaning that the music should be played at a very loud, strong level.

Mezzo forte is an Italian word that means moderately loud. This dynamic level indicates that music should be played with a strong sound, but one step lower than forte. Mezzo forte is often considered to be a normal playing level, whereas forte is the dynamic level where you give it your all. However, forte should never be played in a way that sounds like blasting. Much like accents, remember to never play so loudly that you over blow the note or cause your tone to suffer.

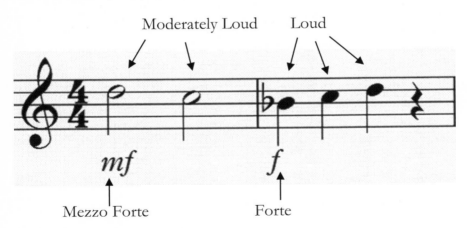

Once a dynamic marking appears in the music, it remains until there is a change. For example, the mezzo forte above would hold true for both the D and C in the first measure, and then would change to forte in measure 2 until otherwise notated.

Soft dynamic levels: **piano and mezzo piano**. Similar to the previous dynamics, piano and mezzo piano are indicated in music as either p or mp. Piano is the Italian word for soft. Music at a piano dynamic level should be played very quietly. This is the softest dynamic level of the four.

Mezzo piano is the Italian word for moderately soft. Music at a mezzo piano dynamic level should be played quietly, but not quite as quiet as piano. Mezzo piano is one step louder than piano, but still considered to be a quiet dynamic.

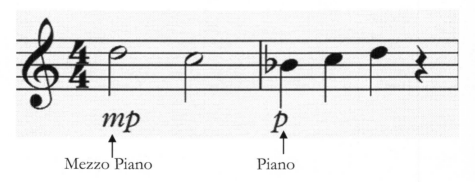

Another form of dynamics are markings that indicate the music should gradually get louder, or gradually get softer. The two dynamic markings that indicate this are called **crescendos and decrescendos**. A crescendo or decrescendo can appear for anything from two notes, to entire lines of music. A crescendo indicates that you will gradually get louder, and a decrescendo indicates that you will gradually get softer. These dynamics typically appear in music as symbols.

Gradually get softer   Gradually get louder

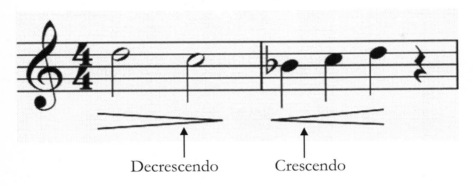

Decrescendo   Crescendo

These dynamics always begin with the very first note in which they appear. A crescendo means that you will gradually get louder as you play each note that it encompasses. This means that if the crescendo takes place between just three notes, you will need to increase your volume very quickly. If it takes place between three measures of music, you will need to increase volume much more slowly. The same is true for a decrescendo and the rate at which you decrease volume.

Listening Example #13: Crescendo and Decrescendo

https://soundcloud.com/jason_randall/sets/how-to-play-the-flute

In track 13, listen to the example above. Take note of the decrescendo in the first measure, and crescendo in the second. Next, listen to the Bb scale played with a rescendo on the way up, and then a decrescendo on the way down.

Crescendo and decrescendo may also be abbreviated as words: cresc. or decresc. When you see one of these dynamics written in the music in abbreviated form, you can assume that it begins where the word appears and ends at the next dynamic change. This can often mean that a crescendo or decrescendo lasts for multiple measures of music - meaning that you will need to increase or decrease volume very gradually.

Dynamics

- Forte = Loud (*f*)

- Mezzo Forte = Moderately Loud (*mf*)

- Mezzo Piano = Moderately Soft (*mp*)

- Piano = Soft (*p*)

- Crescendo = Gradually Get Louder (<)

- Decrescendo = Gradually Get Softer (>)

Vibrato

The use of vibrato is unique for flute players. While many other instruments use vibrato, like violins and singers, flute players are one of only wind players to use vibrato on a regular basis. Any intermediate and advanced flutist should learn to incorporate vibrato into their sound. Once you have been playing for a little while and are feeling comfortable creating a strong sound in every range on the flute, it is time to begin working on vibrato.

Vibrato usually feels very foreign to flute players as they attempt it for the first few times. Vibrato refers to the wavering sound you hear in the notes produced on a flute. This wavering sound can be created in one of two ways: either using the diaphragm or the throat. Vibrato is most commonly produced using the diaphragm, but some players find it much easier to create using the throat. Attempting to produce vibrato using your throat can very risky, since it is easy to mistakenly constrict the air flow with your throat, causing your tone to suffer.

As you begin to practice vibrato, it is best to start using your diaphragm. Vibrato is created by altering the pressure of the breath. It can be very slow or very fast depending on the style of music. To begin learning vibrato, you will need to practice playing long tones while incorporating short bursts of air. You can think of this almost as if saying "ha ha ha" while you hold out a long tone.

Practice these bursts of air very slowly at first. If executed properly, you will hear a waver in your sound each time you send a burst of air. This waver should occur with no change in embouchure or air support. It is important to maintain a strong, steady sound throughout the note. Use your diaphragm to support these bursts of air and maintain an open and relaxed throat. Your shoulders and any other part of your body should not move when you practice these bursts of air.

Once you are comfortable playing with these slow bursts of air, you can begin to experiment with different speeds. Try practicing the bursts of air in a more rapid succession. Then, practice slowing them down. Once you are able to do this at many different speeds, practice changing notes while maintaining consistent vibrato.

Listening Example #14: Vibrato

https://soundcloud.com/jason_randall/sets/how-to-play-the-flute

In track 14, listen to what vibrato sounds like. Listen as the vibrato is very slow at first, and then gradually increases to a much faster speed.

Vibrato is a technique that takes quite a bit of practice to master and become comfortable with. The goal with vibrato is to become consistent, with the ability to incorporate it into your sound at all times. Advanced flutists often vary the speeds of their vibrato to portray different styles of music, and in order to do so you will need to become very comfortable and consistent with your vibrato.

Trills

Perhaps one of the most exciting intermediate flute techniques is the use of trills. Flute music contains frequent trills, especially as you begin to advance in difficulty level. Playing a trill is often very fun for beginners.

A **trill** is a rapid alternation between two notes. It is notated in music as "tr~". When you see this notation in your music, it means that you will alternate between the note that is written and one note higher.

You will always want to slur the notes in your trill, only tonguing the very first note (the note that is written), and then rapidly changing between the two. Seeing this notation in your music is the equivalent of playing something like this.

Trills occur very rapidly, usually alternating between notes as quickly as possible. If you find that you are unable to change notes very quickly due to an awkward finger position, there is probably a trill fingering to aid the transition. A trill fingering is an alternate fingering for the two notes that will allow you to move just one or two keys very quickly. Trilling between two notes in the middle register (the notes that appear on the staff) is often done easily by just lifting one finger. For example, trilling between F and G (as seen in the example above) can be done by lifting just one finger.

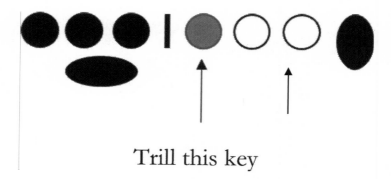

Trill this key

Not all trills will be as easy to complete as this one, so if you find yourself trying to trill between two notes but getting caught up with the finger position, check out a trill fingering chart. You can find most trill fingerings and alternate fingering charts for free online.

Listening Example #15: Trills

https://soundcloud.com/jason_randall/sets/how-to-play-the-flute

In track 15, listen to the Bb scale played with a trill on every note. The trill is completed by rapidly alternating between the current note and the note above.

Chapter 8
Conclusion – Bringing it All Together

Learning to play the flute is a skill you will use for the rest of your life. Whether you play at home for fun, with your friends, at church, or professionally – understanding music is a lifelong skill. Making a sound and getting familiar with the notes is the first step. Once you get comfortable reading music and playing notes on your flute, the possibilities are endless.

With these techniques and strategies, you will be able to play a wide variety of music. Reading this book was a wonderful first step, and while you will likely know more than most other beginners, there is still so much to learn. Should you get to a point in your musicianship where you wish to learn more, or are encountering music with notes and techniques outside what you have learned here, there are a variety of resources you can turn to.

Resources

- Fingering chart

- Tuner

- Flute music books

- Flute websites

Fingering Chart

It is *highly* recommended that you download or purchase a flute fingering chart before you begin playing any music – whether you need it yet or not. Having a full flute fingering chart helps you understand what each key is used for and the differences between all the notes.

If you purchased a flute book, there will likely be a full fingering chart in the front of back of the book. If not, there are a variety of websites which allow you to download a flute fingering chart for free. Here are a couple to start with.

- https://www.amromusic.com/flute-fingering-chart

- https://www.wfg.woodwind.org/flute/

On your phone, the Fingercharts app is available for free download with Android or Apple. This app allows you to look up specific fingerings, including trill and alternate fingerings.

Tuner Resources

Purchasing or downloading a tuner is a great idea for any musician, regardless of their ability level. Getting in the habit of tuning your flute on a regular basis right from the beginning will help you establish great intonation, a sense of pitch, and make tuning significantly easier once you get into more advanced techniques.

Tuners are available for purchase at any music store. There are a wide variety of options, but all tuners accomplish the same thing.

If you decide to purchase a tuner, you may wish to look for one that has a metronome as well. Some more advanced tuners also have an attached microphone, which allows you to tune more accurately if you are in an ensemble setting with multiple people playing.

If you do not wish to purchase a tuner, you can download many different varieties for free on your phone. There are a great deal of tuner apps, and all you have to do is search for them in your app store.

Tuner Apps

- TE Tuner & Metronome

- insTuner

- Chromatic Tuner

Music Books

Once you feel comfortable making a sound on your flute and wish to practice more regularly, purchasing a music book is an excellent choice. There are many beginner flute method books that walk you through learning each note, new rhythms, articulations, dynamics, time signatures and much more. If you are learning on your own without a private teacher, these method books will be a huge help. Some of the most popular method books are:

- Essential Elements

- Accent on Achievement

- Standard of Excellence

- Sound Innovations

If you are studying with a private teacher or in an ensemble, your teacher may have you purchase different etude books or individual solos. A private teacher can help you advance much more quickly than you would on your own, and will be able to help you select enjoyable music that is challenging, yet attainable.

Websites

There are so many online resources that serve to inspire you, answer questions, provide helpful advice, product reviews, audition tips, and a community. If you are passionate about flute playing and want to discover more opportunities and inspiration, I'd highly suggest finding a community or website to help. Here are just a few of the most popular flute websites to get you started.

- http://www.fluteworldblog.com/

- https://www.flutetunes.com/

- https://www.justflutes.com/

- http://thefluteview.com/

- http://www.theflutechannel.com/

This is only the start of your flute playing journey – the possibilities are now endless. Once you begin playing the flute you are joining a community of musicians who serve to inspire, challenge, educate and move others. Enjoy every minute!

If you've enjoyed reading this book, subscribe* to my mailing list for exclusive content and sneak peaks of my future books.

Click the link below:
http://eepurl.com/duJ-yf

OR

Use the QR Code:

(*Must be 13 years or older to subscribe)